The
Everglades
A Timeless Wilderness

Acknowledgements

The publishers wish to acknowledge the invaluable assistance
provided by the following, without whose cooperation the task
of producing this book would have been considerably greater:
Captain's Table Lodge & Villas, Everglades City, Florida.
"Happy Harry's" Scenic Airplane Rides, Everglades City, Florida.
Everglades Canoe Outfitters, Homestead, Florida.
Tim Spalding of Airboat Guide Services, Everglades City, Florida.
Bill Wise of Shark Valley Ranger Station.

Featuring the Photography of J. P. Paireault and Jeremy Thomas
CLB 1477
© 1985 Illustrations and text: Colour Library Books Ltd.,
    Guildford, Surrey, England.
Text filmsetting by Acesetters Ltd., Richmond, Surrey, England.
Printed in Spain.
1985 edition published by Crescent Books, distributed by Crown Publishers, Inc.
ISBN 0-517-47801-3
h g f e d c b a
Dep. Leg. B-44.223-85

The Everglades
A Timeless Wilderness

Text by
Bill Harris

CRESCENT BOOKS
NEW YORK

In the early 16th century, a Puerto Rican Indian named Andreas the Bearded told a Spanish missionary that his father had gone north to the land of Bimini where he found a magic spring that miraculously restored his health and made him look and feel years younger. The missionary was not a gullible man. After all, the Gospel of Saint John had spoken of such a fountain in Jerusalem called Bethesda. According to the Gospel, an angel appeared there once a year to cure the ills of the faithful. This could be history repeating itself on the other side of the world.

A man who believed the story as passionately as anyone was Ponce de Leon, who had arrived with Christopher Columbus on his second voyage to the New World. No one needed such a fountain less than Ponce de Leon who, though fifty years old, was the picture of health. Maybe he thought he could bottle the water and sell it. Maybe he thought finding the fountain would make his name, if not he himself, immortal. If 400 years adds up to immortality, he succeeded. But he never found the magical fountain.

What he found in 1513 was Florida. The Indians had vaguely called everything north and west of Puerto Rico Bimini. But this place, which he thought was a huge island, deserved a more romantic name. A map believed to have been made by Leonardo da Vinci two or three years later used the name Florida for the whole Atlantic coast of what is now the United States. It was an honest mistake. With the possible exception of the silent Norsemen, no European except Ponce de Leon had ever seen any of that coast. Leonardo had to take his word for it.

But if Florida was the first piece of the U.S. known to the white man, there is a piece of Florida they never explored. To some extent, they still haven't. It is the 4,000 square miles of green and brown saw grass and sky blue water known as the Everglades. Possibly the Fountain of Youth is hidden away on one of the thousands of rocky, jungle-covered islands they call "hammocks." They've been there since the Florida peninsula was raised from the sea

some nineteen million years ago, but a huge number of them have never been explored by man. Not even the Indians have seen them all, even though it has been estimated that their ancestors first moved into the Everglades more than two thousand years ago.

The most recent Indian residents are the Seminoles, the descendants of tribes driven by the white man from Georgia, Alabama and the Carolinas, and Indians with ancestral roots in Florida. There are about 1,400 of them living in the Everglades today, and though their roots extend to an assortment of tribes all over the Southeast, they are fiercely proud to be descended from one of the greatest of all the North American Indians, the legendary Osceola.

He was born a Creek in Alabama in about 1804, the same year the Lewis and Clark expedition set out to explore the territory added to the United States by the Louisiana Purchase. He first came to the attention of the white man, and some Seminoles, too, in 1835 at a meeting held at Fort King, near Ocala. The matter being discussed was a new treaty that would require moving the Seminoles from Florida to a reservation in Oklahoma. It was a silly idea from the Indians' point of view. Why would anyone want to move from sub-tropical Florida, where water and game was plentiful, to the open prairies of Oklahoma, fit only for buffalo?

The general in charge had already reported to his superiors that this tribe was troublesome. "They have no intention of fulfilling their treaty stipulations," he wrote, "unless compelled to do so by a stronger force than mere words." He had no idea how true his words would be.

On the appointed day, more than a thousand Indians showed up and camped outside the fort as their leaders went inside to be harangued by the military men. The Seminole spokesman, a tall warrior named Jumper, started the conversation by telling them that his people refused to be moved from their homeland. But there was a treaty to be signed and the representatives of the government in Washington had their orders. After reading it aloud and adding some threatening talk, the general asked the dozen assembled chiefs to make their marks on the paper. Eight of them did, but the other four kept their arms folded. The head chief, Micanopy, was not there. "He is sick," reported Jumper. When pressed about whether the great chief would have signed if he were there, Jumper finally admitted that he would not.

The general's response to that was to cross out five names, including Micanopy's, from the list of required signatures. "These men do not represent the Seminole nation," he said. Then he invited the sub-chiefs to sign and the defeated four joined them. All of them signed except one.

A tall man who had been silently watching the whole sad affair strode forward to the table. He looked the general in the eye and said, "This land is ours! We will not move!" Then, before anyone could move, he pulled his knife from his belt and pinned the treaty to the table. "This is the only way I sign!" he shouted. The American officers, who had grown up revering the words of Patrick Henry, who rallied their country with the words "Give me liberty or give me death," were shocked. This man was a stranger to them. But as he casually walked out of the fort to the cheers of his people, they knew they had not seen the last of Osceola.

He had become a refugee of the Creek War a dozen years before, a victim of Andrew Jackson, the man who, by this year 1835, had become the Great White Father in the White House in Washington. Osceola arrived in Florida as a teenager. He seemed to be a natural leader and, if later accounts of his early years are to be believed, he was able to run farther and faster, hunt more successfully, track more cleverly and outwrestle any Seminole youth. He was also described as unusually handsome and charming, qualities not lost on Seminole girls, who were by just about every account among the most beautiful on the North American continent, red, black or white. Even before he was twenty, he was welcome in the company of chiefs because he and his mother had been prisoners of General Jackson and had taken careful measure of the white men, all of whom he hated passionately.

Ironically, he seems to have earned his living from the white men in his early years. They required Indian guides to help them establish roads and locate communities, and by an earlier treaty agreed that the chiefs should select such guides, who would protect the Indian interests. Osceola must have seemed heaven-sent to them for that purpose. In his travels with surveyors he was paid three dollars a day. But more important, the job taught him more of the ways of the white man and of the land that belonged to his people. His travels also brought him into contact with every pocket of the Seminole nation, and by the time he was ready to lead them to war there was hardly a chief who didn't know him and respect him.

The war didn't begin until several months after Osceola drew his hunting knife at the treaty-signing. The whites didn't believe his threats were really serious, and though their response to the incident was to grant the Seminoles another eight months to get ready to leave Florida, they had no reason to believe the Indians wouldn't eventually go.

Osceola, in fact, was a frequent and welcome visitor at Fort King and was even a very good customer at the store there. They were very happy to sell him all the guns and powder he could afford. But then one day the general came to his senses. He drafted an order prohibiting the sale of lead, powder or guns to any Seminole. Though Osceola had been provisioning his people for war, the order was a hardship to peaceful Indian hunters, most of whom considered the ban a declaration of war.

Osceola confirmed it when he had a violent argument with the Indian agent that ultimately ended with his arrest. It wasn't easy, but the soldiers dragged him off to the guardhouse, where he was placed in irons. His fury became part of his legend. It was said that his shouting was heard deep in the surrounding swamps far into the night. Then suddenly he fell silent, but the quiet was even more ominous.

Everyone knew that though his temper had cooled, his passion had not and that he was silently planning his revenge.

But it seemed otherwise the following morning. He sent a message to the agent that he would not only sign the treaty and follow his people to Oklahoma, but he would convince the other chiefs to do the same.

They didn't know it then, but he had decided to adopt the white man's ways. If they could lie, so could he. The general was so pleased by what he assumed to be a change of heart, that he made Osceola a gift of a fine rifle the day he came to put his mark on the piece of paper.

That fall, Osceola called a secret meeting of his people to make an agreement of a different sort.

All but five of the chiefs, leaders of about 500 Seminoles, agreed to Osceola's edict that any of their people who agreed to move would be considered enemies and were automatically sentenced to death. The five dissenters were allowed to leave, but the rest were bound by the secret pact.

The war itself started about a month later, when an Indian raiding party killed a chief who had begun selling his cattle and making other preparations for the trek west. The following morning a council elected Osceola head war chief with the English-speaking Jumper, and another of the five who had refused to sign the original agreement, a chief named Alligator, as his second-in-command. The murder of the chief alerted the soldiers that trouble was at hand, but their preparations for it were puny compared with Osceola's.

He gave his people a month to relocate in a thick swamp within easy distance of the fort, and he gave himself that same month to teach his warriors how to fight against the white soldiers.

His years of comings and goings within the world of the white man had taught him some valuable lessons. He had noticed, for instance, that cannons were only effective against groups of people. So he told his men to stay as spread out as possible on the battlefield. He had also noticed that it took time to reload after each firing, and deduced that it was during that time that his soldiers should fire back. Watching the white soldiers drill had taught him some things about battlefield discipline, and his became the first Indian fighting force that had rules forbidding sudden rash acts of individual heroism. As their leader he promised them that any brave who didn't follow his orders quickly and without question would be killed on the spot.

He established a network of scouts to watch the enemy's every movement and planned his attacks in places where movement was difficult for wagons and horses and retreat easy for him. He kept his enemies busy on several fronts to keep them off-balance and to keep reinforcements and supplies from getting through.

Of all the Indian armies fought by Americans, none of them, not even the ones who tried to stem the westward tide forty years later, ever matched the discipline of these Seminoles. If the United States Army had sent Osceola to West Point, they couldn't have produced a more formidable adversary.

In the early months of the war he was always at the head of his army of braves, except on one very important occasion. One of their earliest battles was the ambush of a force of 108 men under the command of Major Francis Dade, on a cold December morning in 1835. The Major was the first casualty. Within a matter of less than two hours, all

but four of his men were dead. The Seminoles lost three. Though Osceola had planned the battle, he was not there. The evening before he had been miles away presiding over the death of the Indian agent who had imprisoned him.

After eight months of fighting the Seminoles had never lost a battle. Even the great General Winfield Scott had tried and failed to prove he was a match for Osceola. No one else wanted to try until Richard Call became governor of Florida and announced that he was the Great White Hope. His scheme involved hiring Creek Indians as mercenaries. He issued turbans to them on the theory that one Indian looks like another Indian and he didn't want his men shooting the wrong ones.

Call was the most successful up to that point. He succeeded in destroying some Seminole villages and in driving them deeper into the swamps. The Seminole were at a disadvantage that even their enemy didn't understand. After a year of fighting, they had actually become weary of winning all the time. It was increasingly difficult to get them enthusiastic about going into battle when they knew in advance how the battle would probably turn out. There was no anger, no emotion for revenge, against an enemy who didn't seem to know much about jungle fighting. The tide turned somewhat in the early months of the war's second year. Osceola had contracted malaria and his deputies, Jumper and Alligator, though they understood his tactics, didn't have the same leadership qualities. By spring, they agreed to a truce.

The Seminole were unique among Indian tribes in many ways. One of those ways was that, like their white neighbors, they owned black slaves. Unlike their white neighbors, they had a good relationship with the blacks in their midst, most of whom fought by their side against the white army. They also had free blacks in their midst. When the truce was declared, the Indians agreed to hold more talks about emigrating to Oklahoma and asked the white men to agree to let them take their slaves with them.

But slaves were worth money in that part of the world, and men who earned their living chasing runaways were poised in Northern Florida for what could have been some of the most profitable catches of their careers. The prospect of that kind of sellout brought Osceola out of the swamps again. The truce was over and it was obvious to the white leaders that if they were ever to put an end to the war, they would have to put an end to Osceola first.

They seized their chance the following autumn when the Indian raised a flag of truce over his camp and asked for peace negotiations. His camp was quickly surrounded by soldiers and about 80 of Osceola's people, as well as he himself, were arrested. They were marched to St. Augustine and thrown into prison. The American commander, General Thomas S. Jessup, said in answer to the flood of criticism that Osceola was the one guilty of treachery; that he had violated other promises and that the white flag was really just a red herring. He later said that he arrested the Indians because the 80 warriors with the white flag really intended to attack St. Augustine... which was a fortified city filled with armed soldiers.

The war intensified after that. Late in November, 20 of the Indian prisoners escaped. Osceola, who was either too ill or too proud to take part in the break, remained behind.

Within a month, the remaining prisoners were loaded into a boat bound for Charleston and a more secure prison. General Jessup had meanwhile rounded up about a dozen other Seminole chiefs and some of their followers who had called a truce, but hadn't learned that a white flag didn't mean much to the white man. When the ship sailed north, its passenger list included Osceola, two of his children and his two wives. Also aboard were four Seminole chiefs, 116 warriors and more than 80 women and children.

They weren't treated badly in their prison at the edge of Charleston harbor, but they were far from home and from the war that had dominated their lives for two years. As for Osceola, he had less than five weeks to live. In a final gesture of defiance, he asked to be dressed in full war regalia during his last hour of life. He was buried in Charleston with full military honors, an undefeated enemy. He had never surrendered, nor had his people.

The other prisoners at Charleston were moved west as far as Arkansas. The Seminole nation went further south into Florida, where they served notice on General Jessup that they had never signed a peace treaty with the white man and never would. They never have, and they remain to this day technically at war with the United States. It's a peaceful war, of course, but the fighting didn't end with the death of Osceola.

He had bound them together as a nation and shown them that the white man's army wasn't invincible. He had given them the idea that their homeland was worth defending. Their homeland kept shrinking, to be sure, as the war dragged on. Many went off to the new land in Oklahoma, but several hundred vanished into the Everglades in the mid 1850s. In 1858, a high government official finally admitted that the Seminoles had "completely baffled the energetic efforts of our army to effect their subjugation and removal." By then, other Indians in other places occupied the white man's attention and the Seminole vanished from sight and from memory until 1927, when the Tamiami Trail was finally opened after nearly a dozen years of construction, and automobiles penetrated the Everglades for the first time.

In the nearly 70 years between, the Indians carefully avoided contact with any white men out of fear that they might be loaded on ships and sent away. They lived by hunting and fishing and later by raising cattle. Though they still aren't completely "Americanized," and proudly remember the lessons Osceola taught them, some of them have abandoned the traditional dugout canoes for faster, propeller-driven airboats. Many who have moved to settlements near to the highway have established trading posts where they sell arts and crafts. Others serve as guides to visitors who want to penetrate the Everglades beyond the Trail, and still others operate restaurants and camp grounds for people who want to linger a while. Some have even taken jobs in factories in the area. But none has lost the spirit of independence, and even today it is unusual for groups of Seminoles to enter a white man's building because of what happened to Osceola.

But the young people among them, though not forgetting their traditions, are learning the white man's language, something unthinkable to their grandparents, and adapting to the white man's ways. Nothing is unchanging. Not even the Everglades.

The Everglades is a river. Like any other river, it drains water from higher to lower elevations, in this case from the lower end of Lake Okeechobee to the upper end of Florida Bay. It is only 100 miles long, which takes it out of competition with such rivers as the Mississippi or even the Suwannee. But, at 50 to 70 miles wide, not many of the world's rivers come close to it in size. There is another important difference between the Everglades and other rivers that make it seem like an impostor. In its entire length, it drops just 17 feet to sea level, an average of about three inches per mile. It's obviously not very good for white water rafting. In fact the water flows so slowly it seems to be standing still.

In addition to the water spilling out of the lake, the natural flow through the Everglades comes in the form of some 55 inches of rain each year. More than 35 inches fall during the summer and early fall and by October as much as 90 percent is, according to nature's plan, covered by water. But by the end of August, the situation is traditionally reversed and 90 percent of the land is exposed. The depth of the water, which averages less than two feet even in the rainy season, can be counted on to double in the late summer.

Hurricanes and droughts have changed nature's basic plan many times, but nothing nature has done in 10,000 years comes close to what man has been able to accomplish in less than 80. Modern engineering has even changed its status as a natural river, because so much of it now flows through canals or is held back by dams. It all began in 1906, during one of the early Florida land booms. Men with a love for the shade of green that colors our money took a look at the rich black dirt south of Lake Okeechobee and their eyes lit up. In less than three years after they persuaded the government to build drainage canals they had created more than 1500 profitable farms. The levees, 47 miles of them on the lake alone, and the locks and dams, were called "flood control." But in 1926 and again in 1928 nature reclaimed much of her lost territory in the wake of severe hurricanes.

In the 1930s the federal gvernment infused new money, and an even more ambitious drainage project created even more dry land than the first. But it turned out they did their job too well. They don't get hurricanes every year in Florida. Some years they get droughts. After long periods without rain, some of the new farmland began to resemble a dust bowl. In years with bad storms, the farmers had to fight floods. It took all the profit out of farming and made a lot of people wonder if all those millions of dollars it had cost to drain the Everglades was money well spent.

The government responded the way any good government would. They spent more money. But this time they had more in mind than keeping farmland productive. The cities of Palm Beach and Miami, Fort Lauderdale and Hollywood were growing by leaps and bounds in these post World War II years and needed millions of gallons of water each day. Much of it comes from underground wells, but as more progress came to the area, water needed to be diverted to keep the water table fresh. They had had plenty of warning. In just 15 years from 1909, the underground water west of Miami had turned salty and undrinkable for more than three miles inland.

The problem has been slowed considerably by the project, but people concerned with the future say that by the turn of the next century every drop of rain that falls over a 500 square-mile area will have to be saved just for the population of Dade County. Considering that nature herself takes back 80 percent of the water through a process the scientists call evapotranspiration, it's obvious the engineers will have plenty of work to do over the next several decades. Evapotranspiration, by the way, means that a lot of water evaporates, and that the plants and trees put more mosture into the air through their leaves. It all adds up to humidity. They've got a lot of that in the Everglades.

With all that tampering with nature, we should probably be grateful that any of it has been preserved. The man we should be most grateful to for that is Ernest Francis Coe, a landscape architect who worked for nearly 20 years to turn the Everglades into America's only tropical national park. In the process, he gave up his business, lost his savings and very nearly lost his life.

Coe migrated to Miami during one of the 1920s land booms. It was a golden opportunity for a landscape architect but, as often happened in Florida between the wars, the boom was more hype than opportunity. When it ended, he decided to stay and explore the countryside. What he found was the Everglades. In one of his little tours he found a grove of orchid plants with more than a thousand flowers. He knew at that moment he'd never go home to New England again.

Back in those days, the only white men in the Everglades were hunters and fishermen, and fugitives from justice who were certain nobody would ever go to the trouble to find them.

Coe became a familiar figure to many of them, though luckily they generally considered him harmless. They were sure he wouldn't live very long because he never carried a gun and never wore high shoes to protect himself from rattlesnakes and water moccasins. He didn't even seem too concerned about mosquitoes, though he did carry an old pillow-case to put over his head when he camped out, which was often. On one of those nights he said that something that seemed to be a big cat sat on his shoulder for ten minutes. It didn't seem unfriendly and eventually moved away, but he never got a look at it.

But he loved everything he did see, and decided it should be preserved as a national park. He explored the territory for nearly a year on foot, by boat and even by airplane whenever he could cajole Coast Guard pilots to bend the rules a bit.

He spent the next several months at the drawing board making maps and proposals. During all that time he didn't mind telling anyone who would listen about his dream. Unfortunately, most of the Floridians he talked with thought it was a terrible idea. It was good hunting country and quite a few of the Good Ole' Boys who had made the Everglades their private preserve didn't like the sound of a plan that would protect the animals they loved to hunt.

Many of them threatened to shoot Coe "accidentally" if they should meet him in the Glades. But, fortunately for him, and for us, none ever did.

In 1928 Coe went to Washington with his data and his maps and made an appointment with the Department of the Interior. They had seen hundreds of proposals for national parks since Yellowstone had been suggested in 1872 and had only taken 26 of them seriously. But Coe seemed like a harmless old man to them, too. His presentation turned out to be what one official later said was the best-outlined plan that had ever been put forward for any park. They were also impressed by the idea that this park had features unique not only in the United States, but in the world. And the final advantage was that this park, if approved, would be the only one that could be kept open for visitors all year.

He got their enthusiastic backing. The story should have ended there for Ernest Coe, and he should have lived happily ever after. Actually, it was only the beginning.

His next step was to get Congress to authorize funds to set up a special committee to investigate his idea. Apparently the prospect of investigative trips to Florida appealed to the conferees and President Coolidge signed the authorization just minutes before he left the White House to watch the inauguration of President Herbert Hoover.

Coe spent the rest of the winter playing host to Senators and scientists who explored the Everglades from the gondola of a Navy blimp. They chartered boats, too, but the blimp was much more fun, not to mention safer and mosquito-free.

The hearing didn't last long, and the committee approved the plan without a dissenting vote. But that isn't the same thing as Congressional approval. The next step was to get a bill through the entire Congress authorizing the federal government to accept the Everglades as a gift from the State of Florida. There was nothing unusual or unexpected about that. The law requires that any land converted to a national park must be given to the government at no cost and with no encumbrances. It could either be purchased by the state with their tax money or bonding authority or through public subscription.

Once the Congress agreed to accept the gift, Coe's attention turned to his fellow Floridians, most of whom gave him the cold shoulder. The state chose to go the public subscription route to buy land it didn't already own. Hunters and trappers weren't at all interested. Farmers thought draining was the best thing that could happen to the Everglades. People interested in the tourist business wondered why, if Florida was to have a national park, it couldn't be located farther north where it would be easier for tourists to visit. A lot of other people simply didn't care and, unfortunately for Coe, the list included several governors, one of whom finally disbanded the Florida Everglades National Park Commission altogether.

In the 1930s, some oil companies decided to do some exploration under the Everglades and that made the real estate speculators sit up and take notice. Hunters, meanwhile, had discovered the airplane and developed the airboat which made their "sport" ever so much more fun. People who can't resist picking flowers to stick behind their ears had managed to strip away much of the accessible orchid growth. And, of course, farms and factories had replaced a great deal of the acreage in the northern section of Coe's planned park.

The situation dragged on until 1946, when Governor Millard Caldwell reestablished the commission and forged a compromise. Coe's plan had called for a 2 million acre park, the revised plan stripped it down to 1.4 million acres, about one-seventh of the total area of the Everglades.

Though most of the land had already been acquired by the state, the remaining portion, which had been in the hands of 157 private owners, suddenly belonged to 217 different people and the number was growing as fast as a real estate salesman could talk.

The commission put an end to the speculation by what lawyers call a "declaration of taking," which allowed the state to acquire the land by condemnation immediately, with the price to be settled after the fact by the courts. The plan went into effect when the state put $2 million in escrow against those settlements and transferred the check to the Department of the Interior.

It all became official on June 20, 1947, eighteen years after Ernest Coe made his first trip to Washington to start the ball rolling. The new park was dedicated on December 6 by President Harry S. Truman. Ernest Coe was not an official participant. He never could get used to the idea that his plan had been cut so much and had taken so long.

Coe may have had a good reason to be miffed. The history of Florida is laced with stories of land booms, and during the years Coe was fighting for his park, real estate people were prowling the territory with profit in mind. The result was that by the time the state finally acted, all that was left was land everyone considered worthless except for use by the Indians. That didn't stop them from buying and selling it, though, which is why the special "declaration of taking" needed to be invoked. But the end result was that only 2,300 square miles of the original Everglades were within the boundaries of the National Park. It should also be pointed out that 1,345 square miles were later included in the Everglades Flood Control District, which was created in 1949. A government press release issued at the time included a map of the area with the words "1,345 Square Miles of Alligator and Deer." The release itself explained that "preservation and enhancement of fish and wildlife are among the benefits evaluated for Congress." The park also extends beyond the natural Everglades, adding coastal variety to the experience. And the total experience it provides is nothing less than the biggest sub-tropical wilderness in the United States.

But in the beginning there were people who felt that the park was more than big enough. After all, they pointed out, many people who visited the park in its early years never left the Tamiami Trail. Most never even left their cars except to shop for souvenirs. If that was really true, where would the history of the Everglades have taken us without the Tamiami Trail?

Back in 1898, *The National* a popular magazine of the day, sent its correspondent, Mr. Freeman Furbush, to Florida to have a look around. He hopped down the East Coast observing "the million dollar tourists who find life a burden because of their riches." He also found a lot of "those land-scheme 'shysters' who steal your good money for a bad investment."

Of those he said, "They are suave, servile and sanctimonious fellows who, amid the luxury of a hotel smoking-room, will tell you that this is a land flowing with milk and honey and that, of course, if you happen to have a few thousand lying around waiting to be judiciously invested, why, here is your chance. Nothing safer, nothing surer. So you close the deal and kiss your money goodbye. Later, when the papers have been passed, you journey into the wilderness somewhere and after knocking about for a week or two, finally reach your Eldorado only to discover that your kiss was well-placed, that instead of a land of milk and honey, you are the proud possessor of a land of sand and snakes."

His fellow tourists, he said, were mainly "gorgeously-dressed women who tiptoe through Florida on high-heeled French shoes in search of the cure for an ailment they never had. They are the wives and daughters of our wheat, cotton, iron and oil kings, and the kings themselves, who take their regular Turkish baths, their 'round the hotel constitutional,' their mineral water drinks and their stylish doctor's medicines.

"Invalids, every one of them. Invalids who order chicken livers en brochette for breakfast, boned capon aux trufee at luncheon, and for dinner supreme de volaille, a la reine, haricots verts. These invalids retire at midnight and write North and tell in their dainty lavender-scented notes how much, how wonderfully much, 'this really divine climate is doing for me down here.'"

His journey finally took him to Miami, "the extreme southern point in the United States reached by rail." Of course, that fact would change, but at this point in 1898, "Mr. Flagler, the Standard Oil Millionaire and greatest capitalist-benefactor of Florida has just completed the last jewel in his costly necklace of hostelries, the Royal Palm."

After a week in this "American Naples," Furbush decided to move on. "We went across Florida to the West Coast," he said, "where Mr. Plant, like Mr. Flagler on the East Coast, has invested millions of dollars in hotels, railroads and tourist attractions. I wanted to go into the Everglades for a spell and see what a first-class swamp was like. But my traveling companion said he was afraid of the Seminole Indians, so I humored his whim and instead of taking up a wigwam went straight to Tampa Bay and engaged a room at the modern Alhambra there. It was furnished with divans that once graced the Tuilleries and a push-button arrangement whereby you could call for anything from a thousand dollars to a glass of manufactured ice water."

It was obvious that the young men in their white ducks and the ladies in their high-heeled shoes would soon clamor for a better way to get from Miami to Tampa without the bother of going around the Everglades. The trip took two days.

The road that reduced the journey to less than two hours was the brainchild of Captain J.F. Jaudon, who in 1916 had accumulated land near his hometown of Ochopee and planned to build a new town.

The first white men had crossed the Everglades back in 1857, when an expedition was led by an Indian woman named "Old Polly." She had crossed the Glades alone from east to west in 1839 and when Captain Jacob Mickler and his force of 124 men needed to join forces with Captain Abner Doubleday (the man who later took credit for inventing the American game of baseball, not to mention founding a publishing company), they hired Polly to guide them. The 1857 trek took them from Fort Myers to Biscayne Bay.

It was such a harrowing experience that nobody bothered to try it again until James Ingraham led a party of surveyors from the Cypress Swamps to the Bay in 1892. Their mission was to find a route for a railroad. Their report called it impossible. But when a railroad was built from Homestead to Key Largo in 1907, men like Jaudon began to wonder if the Ingraham report was all it was cracked up to be.

After he surveyed a possible route, Joudon got a $125,000 contract from Dade County and went to work. By 1923 all he had to show for his work was a rough road that went 60 miles to nowhere. Meanwhile, Lee County had appropriated $355,000 and sent out some dredges to begin a road from the West Coast. At the same time, a motorcade of ten cars, 23 men and a pair of Indian guides left Fort Myers on April 4, 1923 to prove that it was possible to drive a car across the Everglades. They could have gone around it in less time. The trip took three weeks, much of the time spent trying to find the way. All the people made it, but three of the cars didn't. They proved their point though. Almost no one in America hadn't heard about the Tamiami Trail after that, and even if the state hadn't already committed itself to improving Florida's roads, this one would have had to have been built.

But there were times over the next five years when anyone would have understood if they just gave up and quietly walked away from it.

It seemed relatively easy in the beginning. The plan called for dumping rock over the top of the mud. But when it rained, the rocks sank. When it didn't rain for long periods they sank anyway, because the dried out mud often burned away in the fires that became an Everglades trademark after the first efforts to drain it.

The only way to build a road that would last longer than it took to build it was to dig out all the muck down to the limestone base and cover that with rock. It took millions of sticks of dynamite to do the job. It also took a huge toll in lives lost to explosions, to snakes, to drowning. The first men in the chain of progress had to work in chest-high water, cutting away the underbush and tough saw grass, all the while keeping out a watchful eye for water moccasins. They were followed by crews who built a temporary log road to carry in the drilling machines and supplies. The dynamite was brought in on ox carts, many of which slipped into the water and had to be righted by human muscle-power. Mosquitoes followed them every step of the way.

The next step was giant dredges that dug a canal along the right of way, throwing the rock and mud into the base of the road. The whole project was finally finished on April 25, 1928, nearly a dozen

years and $13 million after it began. In the best of times it never inched forward more than two miles a month. The name "Tamiami" is not a cute way of saying that the road goes to Miami. It is a combination of the names Tampa and Miami, the cities it connects. Cuteness was to come later with a more modern road, the two-lane Everglades Parkway, a toll road between Naples and Fort Lauderdale, which is called "Alligator Alley."

The year the Tamiami Trail opened, the fourth killer hurricane in six years blew in from the west on September 16. It was the worst storm civilized man had ever seen in Florida.

Old-timers say that the 1928 storm raised the water level in the Everglades from four to eight feet in less than an hour. There are water marks in some buildings that were spared that show the flood reached as high as 25 feet. Two hundred people running from their homes in Belle Glade at the southeastern corner of Lake Okeechobee were all drowned before they could reach safety. Before the day was over some 2,400 people were dead. But it was weeks later before anyone dared to make an estimate. Bodies were collected and burned, and many families had no idea what became of relatives and friends who ran ahead of the storm and were never seen again.

Hundreds of alligators were drowned, and thousands of fish were tossed from the lake onto dry land. Many farms were washed away with all of their livestock. Homes had vanished as completely as their occupants.

Lake Okeechobee and the Everglades would never be the same again. But the changes that began that day in 1928 weren't as much a matter of nature healing her wounds as man preventing them from happening again.

With the help of the federal government, a massive flood control project was begun near the end of 1930. By expanding the St. Lucie and Caloosahatchee Canals, an old dream of a water route across Florida was finally realized, though many complained it was too far south to do any good.

The first vessels to make the trip across the 155-mile waterway in 1937 was a flotilla that was met at every stop by feasting and fanfare. In its first two months more than 3,000 small boats made the trip from Stuart to Fort Myers.

But what they saw along the way was not as beautiful a sight as they would have seen a decade before. The project had produced a levee, 40 feet high in some places, along the south shore of Lake

Okeechobee. From the lake itself it had become impossible to see the towns and farms below it, not to mention the Everglades, as had once been possible. The winding Caloosahatchee River had its heart torn out by dredges that straightened out its curves by ripping up groves of cypress and oak and unceremoniously dumping debris along its banks.

The whole thing cost more than $19 million. In return, the Florida farmers got some properous land, the average level of the lake was reduced by five feet and no subsequent hurricanes, not even the terror of 1947, have been able to change it again. Railroads began serving the east and south sides of the lake and another highway was cut across the Everglades, connecting Fort Lauderdale with Okeechobee.

The project also cut the flow of water from the lake into the Everglades. Fires that destroyed dried-out muck became more and more common. Acre after acre of sawgrass turned brown and fueled more fires. Meanwhile, the Great Depression had ended and Florida was feeling the effects of another boom. Along the East Coast farms sprang up as far inland as the new north-south highway and the New River Canal, on land once considered worthless. More farms and even retirement communities filled other reclaimed land toward the West Coast. Meanwhile, the Everglades, like the Seminole all those years before, has retreated south.

The Everglades owes its life to the great Lake Okeechobee which, except for Lake Michigan, is the largest fresh water lake in the United States. Its shoreline is 135 miles around and a boat trip across it is about 31 miles long. It is also among the shallowest of America's big lakes. Even in the rainy season it is less than 20 feet deep.

In the 1860s, the plains west of the lake became cowboy country, with huge herds of cattle destined to feed the Confederate Army. It took 40 days to drive the cattle north to the Georgia border, and in the first two years of the Civil War more than 25,000 steers made the trip, which made the area around Fort Myers a strange little battlefield miles removed from the big war further north. Even then, the population of Florida had a strong mixture of people who had migrated from the North and during the unpleasantness of the '60s, the Union Army occupied the fort on the Gulf and found plenty of willing "traitors" (they preferred to call them "refugees") in the local population to keep the Confederate Cavalry off balance. Richmond responded by ordering that all able-bodied men over 17 and under 50 were required to serve in the Army, with the result that the cattle herds kept going north, even though the Yankees did everything they could to make the trip a hard one.

After the war, the cattle industry boomed in Southern Florida because of another war. The Cubans had decided to fight for their independence from Spain and, during the ten years the rebellion lasted, Florida steers provided meat for both sides who, unlike the Confederacy, paid cash on delivery.

The cowboys who rounded up the steers didn't work in quite the same way as their glamorous counterparts out West. They relied less on horses, partly because their ranges were smaller and partly because of the abundance of mosquitoes and flies that distracted them. Instead of lassoes, they used long bull whips to rope their calves. Many of them had migrated from Georgia, where such whips had long been a symbol of status. Men traditionally carried the long whips if for no better reason than to crack them to announce their presence, and their presumed superiority. To them, to be called a "cracker" was a sign of respect.

But if their range land was limited, there was plenty of territory to be exploited and the fun began in the 1880s, when Henry Flagler began developing the peninsula's East Coast and Henry Plant started acquiring the West. In the center, the northern part of the Everglades, an influential Pennsylvanian named Hamilton Disston became the largest single landowner in the entire United States when he paid 25 cents an acre for four million acres of very wet land below Lake Okeechobee.

The state had previously speculated itself into a corner and was forced to sell the land it owned. Many Floridians were opposed to the deal. The price was too low, in the opinion of some. Others were scandalized by the fact that some of the land wasn't even under water. Still others couldn't help wondering if the small army of squatters there wouldn't be justly compensated for the land they were squatting on.

Part of Disston's agreement was that the land must be drained and reclaimed. Within three years he had converted about half of it to dry land. He had already sold farmland at as much as $5 an acre and within a half-dozen more years, the same land was resold at $20 an acre. His development included research on the feasibility of growing rice and potatoes, sugar cane and peaches. But his plans were nipped in the bud when he died in 1896, leaving about two million acres of Florida land worth some $2.2 million. His heirs weren't at all interested in continuing his enterprise and Central Florida went back to sleep again. At the beginning of the new century, the population of Southern Florida below Lake Okeechobee was less than two people per square mile.

The Flagler railroad interests, which had been given huge tracts of land to encourage development, took over where Disston left off. They hired experts to help fledgling farmers and Henry Flagler personally guaranteed loans to farmers whose crops were sometimes destroyed by unexpected frosts. When the railroad reached into the interior just after the turn of the century, they began running special excursion trains to farms that were offered for sale only to buyers who had actually seen them.

This un-Floridian gesture was cancelled out in 1905 when the new Governor Napoleon Bonaparte Broward convinced the legislature that the future of Florida depended on the untold wealth of a drained Everglades. What they needed to make the dream come true was another dreamer with a million dollars to invest. Broward found his man at the Democratic National Convention in Denver in 1908. While other delegates were concentrating on nominating William Jennings Bryan to be their party's standard-bearer, Brower did his politicking with Richard J. Bolles, a New Yorker who had gone far enough fast enough to have acquired his own seat on the New York Stock Exchange before he was twenty-three years old.

But Wall Street was too tame for him. He wandered west, where he made and lost fortunes in mining ventures. Then he decided there was more money to be made in the land itself than what was under it. He proved it by turning a profit of more than $2 million selling farms on an Oregon mountainside. By 1908 he was looking for new worlds to conquer and Governor Broward suggested that the Everglades might represent such a challenge.

The governor had already started construction of a hundred-mile canal from Fort Lauderdale to lake Okeechobee, and desparately needed money to finish it. Sight-unseen, Bolles bought 500,000 acres of underwater land for a million dollars. He had bought the land in Oregon sight-unseen, too. The difference between the two was that the Oregon mountainside was high and quite dry. In Florida it was officially termed "over-flowed land."

In Oregon, the pitch to buyers was based on promises of dams and irrigation canals. In Florida the promise was less empty. His contract with the state specifically earmarked two dollars an acre for drainage and reclamation.

Other speculators also bought Everglades land from the Brower administration, but few were as imaginative in the resale as the variety of companies established by Mr. Richard J. Bolles.

His confederates were a Missouri lawyer and a couple of Kansas City real estate operators who had proved their value to him in the far west. Like Bolles himself, none of them had ever been to Florida. It didn't make much difference to them. Neither had their prospective customers.

For their first trick, they marked off 180,000 acres on a map of Dade and Palm Beach Counties. After dividing it into 12,000 farms, three quarters of which were less than ten acres, they dropped a town into the center. The town's name, they said, would be "Progresso." It would have 12,000 (a magic number that had worked in Oregon where Bolles sold 12,000 farms) building lots, as well as broad streets, churches and factories.

It was all to be sold under individual "Contracts" that would cost a buyer about $250 payable in monthly instalments of $10 each. All any buyer knew was that the contract was good for one farm of undetermined size, and a town lot of unspecified location.

Once enough contracts were sold, an auction was held to determine the actual distribution of the land. It was all very democratic. The auction was held by "trustees" elected by the contract holders. And it was all just confusing enough to make a salesman's job easy.

To make it even easier for the boys in the Sales Department Bolles had enough political clout to get access to an unreleased government survey that showed the land in question was not only below the frost line, but was rich enough to eliminate the need for fertilizers. It was all very official-looking, and in the hands of the right salesman it looked like the land companies had complete government backing.

That was a strong incentive to the government workers and the midwest farmers as well as teachers and other middle-class people the salesmen managed to ferret out. The idea of a new life in sunny Florida was an easy one to sell, too. The pitch was clinched with a guarantee of $1000 plus expenses to anyone who could prove that the farm land wasn't as good as the promises made in any "printed literature." It was the verbal promises that were unbelievable.

Between 1908 and 1912, more than 50 operators offered similar schemes. The Secretary of Agriculture was quoted by one of them as saying that "the Everglades affords promise of development which reaches far beyond the limits of prophecy." Nobody bothered to point out that the statement had been made, and discredited, nearly 20 years earlier and that the man was dead and couldn't explain what he had been trying to say. On the other hand, a very much alive William Jennings Bryan, recently defeated for the third time in the race for the Presidency, said: "I regard the reclamation of the Everglades as one of the greatest enterprises on record. One could hardly believe that there was such an enormous wealth of undeveloped soil in America and the area of the tract is amazing." There is no record of Mr. Bryan having put any of his money where his mouth was.

Meanwhile, like many other big public works projects, the drainage program became bogged down in politics. The state commissioner didn't get along with the land speculators and the railroad interests didn't get along with either one. In 1911 a Congressional hearing was called to investigate the Department of Agriculture, which had been accused of covering up an unfavorable Everglades report. A year later a Congressman from Missouri asked for an investigation of what he called "one of the meanest swindles ever devised or conducted anywhere in this country." The swindlers he was referring to were the cohorts of Richard Bolles, one of whom had become a United States Attorney.

Many of the company's customers had already banded together to take Mr. Bolles to court, but legal fees were in many cases nearly as high as the $250 they had lost by listening to the salesmen. Bolles was finally sued by the Post Office for fraudulent use of the mails. But to stand trial they needed to extradite him to Kansas City, where his company was chartered, The 74 year-old Bolles died aboard the train that was taking him from Palm beach to the Midwest to answer for his so-called crimes.

Though he had his enemies and victims as well, a lot of people regarded Bolles as the savior of their lives. Dozens of new towns were established in parts of the Everglades where the drainage program was successful, even though "Progresso" was never built. And though they fought frost and burning muck and had to invent new tricks to make the land produce, the rich farms they established would have defied the words of even the most enthusiastic promoter. In one of his trials Bolles defended himself by pointing out that he had only believed what he had been told by public officials and that he himself had been gulled by a false promise. In defense of the politicians, no one had any idea how tough it would be to drain the Everglades. And as one of them pointed out, "anybody who buys land he has never seen is a damn fool." There were more than 25,000 such people who invested in the Everglades in those four short years. But the families of hundred of them are there now having the last laugh.

On the other hand, there are many people who think that what man has done to the Everglades isn't at all funny. They look at the bird known as the Everglades kite, which has inherited a finicky appetite from its ancestors, who decided eons ago that the only thing worth eating is the little apple snail. The snail's ancestors decided about the same time that the only place to live was the Everglades. But since the Everglades is now about half the size it was at the turn of the century, there aren't as many apple snails as there used to be. The kite, meanwhile, had developed a hook in its beak that's great for getting apple snails out of their shells but not much else. There are less than 100 Everglades kites left in the world. Man never hunted them, never had anything against them, in fact. But if man had never invaded the Everglades, there would be thousands of Everglades kites wheeling and diving for unsuspecting snails right this minute.

In spite of the fact that the population of man-eating insects will always be thousands of times greater than the human population, mankind seems hell-bent on trying to even things up. And for every person who decides Florida is a nice place to live, there are dozens who are discovering it's a wonderful place to visit.

One visitor wrote in his diary: "What a change has been made in this place in the last year! From two houses, it has been made a town of two thousand. Its splendid new hotel with every modern convenience will lure the tourist, but for me the picturesqueness seems to have gone; the wilderness has been rudely marred by the hand of civilization." The entry was made in the winter of 1897.

In 1947, when the destruction of growth was already apparent, Marjory Stoneman Douglas made America sit up and take notice in her book *The Everglades: River of Grass*. After describing the devastating droughts of the mid-40s, she wrote: "The fall rains of 1945 put out the fires. The people, all those diversified masses of people who lived in this sunny and beautiful country, by the great sea, under the silken and moving airs, in a land that was still green with trees and gardens and growing groves, forgot. The old wastefulness went on. The bulldozers of new lot owners destroyed the hardwood trees of ancient cut-up hammocks. In the Big Cypress the lumber companies were cutting out the tallest of the ancient gray trees. A new wave of hungry life, after the war, moved down into the sun and the expanding coastal cities. Again, the life and death of the Everglades went unrecognized."

Her book was as important as Rachel Carson's *Silent Spring* in making the country aware of the importance of preserving what nature has given us. Soon after the book appeared, she formed an organization called Friends of the Everglades which has been attracting like-minded persons to the cause ever since. In an interview summing up her experiences as a Floridian for 70 years, she said: "It has been like going over Niagara Falls in a barrel. You were just hurtled along by the force and impetus of this population. It's come in waves of boom and bust. It's nothing but the climate. Yet they come down here and live in air-conditioned condominiums and they don't know anything about the country or the tropics or what the country is like. And out of sheer weight of ignorance, they're destroying the whole business.

"The whole area is just this narrow strip of land around the wetlands. You can have houses around the edges, but you can't put them where the water is. If you build there and drain it, you won't have any more water."

Well into her 90s, she has been called an old fuddy-duddy and a butterfly lady. But she has history on her side, and the history shows that man himself may be in as much danger in southern Florida as the birds and beasts.

Though the traditional view is that the source of the Everglades is Lake Okeechobee, the lake itself is fed by the Kissimmee River, which drains a system of lakes as far north as Orlando. The river has always been prone to widespread flooding in the wet season, and the march of civilization handled the problem in 1962 by diverting it into a canal with the unglamorous official name of C-38, and the popular name of Kissimmee Ditch. The system of dikes and dams that make the ditch an effective flood control vehicle has created rich pastureland and a thriving dairy industry. But it has replaced the once-beautiful river with a creation no lovelier than its official name.

C-38, in addition to carrying pollutants from farms and factories into the shallow lake, has also dramatically changed the way water flows into the Everglades. It is an important link in the chain that has created nearly a thousand square miles of farmland and provided the means of pumping excess water into the 1,345 square-mile Everglades Flood Control District, which has now been divided into three conservation areas. The water stored there is held in reserve to keep the Biscayne Aquifier supplied with fresh water. The aquifer is an underground reservoir that prevents the faucets in Southern Florida condominium kitchens from delivering salt water.

The conservation areas are open to the public for fishing and hunting and camping. But when the third one was finished in 1962, its most prominent feature was an earth dam with a road on top, just long enough to stop any natural flow of water further south than the Tamiami Trail. There are watergates in the dam, but they are kept closed much of the time. They are open, in the words of an official document, "when water levels permit." The translation is "when Lake Okeechobee is at least 12.5 feet above sea level." To many conservationists, another translation is "when Hell freezes over."

The lake is drained near the end of the dry season each year in anticipation of heavy fall rains and possible hurricanes. The water is pumped out to sea. When the Everglades needs it most, it simply isn't available.

For all their careful planning, and the millions of dollars they have spent, the engineers can't seem to simulate the rhythms of nature. Though they have been trying to tame the Everglades since the middle of the 19th century, they haven't pleased everybody yet.

They keep digging ditches and draining more land, but in the process, they have eliminated underground water along with the surface water. The rainy season water level within the confines of Everglades National Park, where there is never a thought of draining and reclaiming, has dropped about five feet in the last hundred years. In half that time, the depth of the fertile soil in the land they've reclaimed has been reduced by the same five feet through oxidation. Some people, the farmers call them alarmists, say that the rest wil be gone by the first decade of the next century.

The reduced water table has made alarmists of the developers themselves, who know that a housing development or a factory can't survive long without fresh water. But they keep on building them, keeping their fingers crossed, no doubt.

Meanwhile, the Army Corps of Engineers, who took over the project in the 1950s, tells everyone not to worry. The director of the program has said they are restudying the problem "to make it even more effective in meeting the critical and difficult water problems here." That was not very long after the director of the National Park Service had said, "We did not acquire this subtropical wonderland to let it go by default. But if we don't act promptly and wisely, we'll have a dried-up mud flat on our hands."

While that discussion was taking place, other officials were fighting among themselves over a scheme to improve the quality of life in Greater Miami by building a huge jetport in a reclaimed corner of the Everglades. Mercifully, the project never got off the ground, but the battle raged long enough to be frightening.

There are times when even mother nature herself seems to be conspiring against the Everglades. A part of the natural cycle has always been devastating fires. When water levels drop, the muck dries out and either lightning or oxidation causes it to burn. In the process, old growth is removed and the ashes provide nitrogen-rich soil that encourages new young growth, made possible by more available sunlight. The fires, which often rage out of control for weeks, though frightening and seemingly destructive, are as important as water itself to the future of life in the Everglades. But since humans have become part of the cycle, the cycle has gotten out of control.

In a six-month period in the early 1970s, after the driest winter since record-keeping began, there was an average of one hundred fires a month in the Everglades. Of those 600 fires, less than a dozen were part of the natural process. The rest were caused by people.

In the days when all Everglades fires were natural, there was always water at or just below ground level. Only the tops of the sawgrass and other vegetation burned. But reclamation removed the water and the dried-out muck burned along with the plants and trees. To make matters worse, the muck keeps on smoldering, usually until the next heavy rain, making it impossible for animals to move from place to place for weeks at a time. Long enough for starvation to do what the fire could not.

Meanwhile, the organic matter destroyed in the fires that raged after the drought of 1971 hasn't been replaced yet. It may never be.

The losers, of course, are the creatures that were there first. In less than 40 years, according to some experts, the alligator population has been reduced by more than 90 percent. Poachers cashing in on the market for watch bands, shoes and handbags are responsible for a great deal of the loss, but lack of water would have put the alligator on the endangered list without the additional help.

Though their numbers have dwindled, alligators are still one of the main attractions for Everglades visitors. They are one of the "must-see" attractions all over Florida, in fact. But the alligator has a cousin who lives in Southern Florida, and to see one is a genuine event. They don't like being seen. Crocodiles are so shy, in fact, that biologists didn't know there were any in the United States until about a century ago.

If you should ever meet one, you'll know it isn't an alligator because it will be bigger. Even small ones are a dozen feet long and weigh as much as 500 pounds. If that doesn't frighten you away, you'll notice that the croc has a narrower snout and it has an overbite about a third of the way down. The protruding tooth on each side makes a crocodile look like it is smiling.

Though nesting alligators have been known to attack humans, and others have taken over many a Florida swimming pool while dining on the family pet, crocs have other tastes. Once scientists discovered their existence, they promptly placed them on the endangered species list because they are so hard to find. Though they are indeed endangered, some think that the croc population has hardly changed in a hundred years. But people who keep track of such things aren't sure. The estimate is that there are about 600 crocodiles in the mangrove swamps, but the only way to count them is to take to the swamps at night with a flashlight. The light is reflected back from the beast's eyes and counting is as easy as dividing by two.

Attempts have been made to band them for further indentification. But a nesting female disturbed in any way will wander off and never come back. As farmers and estate builders have moved south, all the crocodiles have been a few steps ahead of them, with the result that the entire population is now concentrated in the extreme south. There is no place left for them to go because they don't like living in temperatures below 70 degrees. Some had been pushed by progress down into the Keys, but as progress reached there, they ambled north again to make a last stand in the Everglades.

Their battle against extinction is normally against raccoons, who have a taste for crocodile eggs, and herons, who think baby crocs are quite a delicacy. The babies, usually hatched in batches of 30 or 40, are carried to the water by their mothers in the first minutes of their lives. The water needs to be fresh or the young ones will dehydrate. But if they get too much too fast, as often happens when the watergates are opened, they drown. It's amazing any of them survive. Less than half do.

American crocodiles are surviving in coastal Central America and on some of the larger Caribbean islands. Its cousin, the alligator, on the other hand, exists only in America, if you discount all those polo shirts and a midget version that roams in China. It qualifies, hands-down, for the title of "Ugly American," with its bulging eyes, its dragon-like feet and horny skin. Though it prefers living in Florida, it ranges as far north as the Carolinas and west to Texas.

Spanish explorers were the first to duck out of their way. They warned their companions when one appeared by shouting "el legardo," which means "the lizard" in English. English-speaking settlers heeded the same warnings but, as is common with English-speaking people, heard the warning as "alligator."

When the Spanish arrived, the warning was heard a lot. It's likely that there were more than 5 million alligators swimming in Florida's ponds and rivers and sunning themselves along the shore back then. No one knows for sure how many are left, but the best guesses put the population in the neighborhood of 500,000. Most of them are in the relative safety of the Everglades, where game wardens and park rangers protect them from poachers, the greatest enemy they have encountered in 200 million years of survival.

Poaching alligators is nothing new in Florida. In the 1880s more than 2.5 million of them were killed, and that was before swamp buggies and high-powered flashlights made the job easy. The methods they used are as inhumane as the clubbing of baby seals up north. Poachers went into the swamps at night with lanterns and long rifles. When the light reflected from an alligator's eyes, it was simple to aim the gun at a spot midway between the two points of light and a good hunter could have the animal skinned before the echo of the shot died in the distance. Others staked out likely dens and dragged the alligator out with a long, hooked pole.

As the years went by, the alligator killers got more sophisticated. Their noisy swamp buggies allow them to get deeper into the Everglades where they can avoid game wardens. Sometimes they even use low-flying airplanes to spot 'gators and to keep an eye peeled for the law. Rather than wasting time hunting, they set big hooks on poles anchored to the bottom of ponds and bait them with chickens or chunks of beef. When an alligator snaps at the bait, the hook snaps back and the creature is trapped until the poacher makes his rounds again.

In the 19th century, the laws against killing alligators weren't as tough as they are today, but poaching is still big business because alligator skins are still very much in demand, at prices that make it worth the risk. An Italian designer recently advertised a pair of men's shoes made of "genuine alligator" for $550, a price considered a bargain.

Though wearing alligator-skin shoes is as conscienceless an act as wearing a leopard-skin coat, the hides the shoe designer is making all that money with are most likely legal. Many alligators are raised on "farms" for such purposes, and the Florida Game and Fresh Water Fish Commission periodically monitors "controlled harvests" in areas where the alligator population seems to be growing too fast. Harvests are open only to qualified hunters, carefully selected and closely watched. The skins they collect are theirs to sell legally.

The Commission also runs a program of relocating animals that residents consider a "nuisance." Though it extends from raccoons to noisy birds, all of which are picked up and moved to less civilized locations, alligators are the most frequent source of nuisance calls, and the most likely not to be moved. The bigger they are, the greater the danger they'll be killed instead. Over the year, "nuisance alligators" account for a fairly large collection of valuable skins, which are sold at auction prices that contribute a great deal to the cost of running the relocation program.

Legal or not, alligator skins are big business, and will be as long as there are people who find self-importance in wearing shoes that cost $550, and other people who get rich catering to their so-called taste. But the race is on to see which species becomes extinct first.

Visitors to the Everglades watch alligators from elevated wooden walkways and from boats where each is safe for the other. Most people are content to watch in silence with a touch of awe, but some persist in tossing soft drink bottles at them to see what happens. Almost no one can resist the human impulse to feed them, an especially interesting experience when the wide mouth opens to display the rows of sharp teeth. Over the years, it has become a custom to toss marshmallows at them because nothing else seems to make an alligator move more quickly. It's a lot like feeding peanuts to an elephant or a peanut sandwich to a bear in Yellowstone. But like the latter, these huge beasts will eat just about anything, including the hand that holds the marshmallow. Also like the Yellowstone bears, big 'gators tend to get bold and beg for handouts. When that happens, the solution is the same as out west: they are rounded up and moved to parts of the park where there are no people to beg from.

Though it would be the height of foolishness to classify an alligator as "harmless," they'll attack and catch any creature that moves except man. A female guarding her nest is best avoided, of course, and there have been rare accounts of attacks on people for other reasons, usually something stupid on the part of the people. But most encounters between the two species are usually more harmful to beast than man.

They have a reputation for being able to move quickly over land for short distances, but they are clumsy out of water and easily escaped. Escape is always the best policy. These huge, eight-to-ten-foot creatures can easily kill full-grown cattle and often do. Their stomach is bigger than their mouth, too. One ten-footer was once observed swallowing three whole pigs in a matter of minutes. Fortunately for pigs and cows, they eat almost nothing in the fall and winter months. But during the rest of the year they never stop eating.

Keeping them well-fed is one of the tricks used by the men who make their living with exhibitions of live alligator wrestling, one of the great local "sports" in Southern Florida. But the most important trick is simply grabbing the animal by its snout so it can't open its jaws. If it should, turning it on its back relaxes an alligator into an almost hypnotic state. But as long as the wrestler doesn't let go, there is almost no danger. Because of that the most important trick of all is to shake the alligator violently to make it appear there is a struggle going on. Usually there isn't. Alligators have few natural enemies and don't need an instinct for fighting.

They have survived from prehistoric times without violence, and their capacity for continued survival is best seen through their little cousins in China, the only other alligators in the world. They have survived centuries of crowded civilization in the lower Yangtze Valley in spite of the fact that the Chinese have always treasured their tough, waterproof hides and have used their intestines as the source of medicines and potions. There are accounts of alligator hunts in China as many as 15 centuries ago, and records older than that suggesting that the dragon, revered by generations of emperors as an omen of good fortune, probably began its long march through Chinese history as an alligator.

Even though many a creature in the Everglades eventually winds up as an alligator's dinner, almost all of them would consider 'gators a source of good fortune. Most wouldn't survive until dinner time without them. They depend on the peculiar living habits that set alligators apart from every other reptile, habits many scientists say are a large part of the proof that alligators are a species virtually unchanged since the age of the great dinosaurs.

Most reptiles, even crocodiles, build nests, lay eggs and go on about their business. 'Gators are homebodies who usually stay in the same dens all their lives and often pass them on from generation to generation. They rarely stray more than a mile or so from the place they were born, and scientists who have studied them report that even when they are moved as many as a dozen miles, they'll eventually find their way home with an instinct that would put a pigeon to shame.

But if they don't change their location often, they are constantly changing their environment. The greatest change comes at nesting time. That job falls to the female, who begins by selecting a likely spot near the den and clearing a space in the brush about ten feet square. She bites off most of the vegetation and pulls the rest up by the roots. The trash she collects is piled in the center of the square with a bulldozer-like motion of her tail. She mashes the pile down by rolling over it, all the while pushing loose material toward the center. When she is satisfied that the mound is high enough she begins using her hind feet, one at a time, to make a hollow in the center. She gets leverage by keeping her front feet firmly planted on the ground.

When the hole seems big enough for the 30 to 70 eggs she'll lay, she puts mouthfuls of mud and waterlogged roots into it. Then she follows up with more mud on the outside to create a four-foot, cone-topped structure. The whole process can take as many as four days and nights, during which time Mrs. Alligator never stops working. Once the job is done, she lays her eggs in the cavity then covers it with more mud and wet roots. Considering the tools at her disposal, the finished nest is a wonder to behold.

To keep admiring raccoons and birds from getting too close, the female 'gator stays near her handiwork for all of the nine weeks it takes for the eggs to hatch. She busies herself during that time by daubing a little mud here and there. Once her eight-inch babies begin making noises inside the eggs, she carefully pulls away the mud and debris and helps them escape into the watery den.

In the process of building her nest, she manages to dig a rather large hole underwater which will protect her babies from herons and raccoons and some turtles, but they'll rely on her to keep fish and water snakes and otters, all of whom think baby alligators are a tasty treat, at arm's length.

But if the lure of a good meal attracts many of the alligator's neighbors, the nest-building process itself provides them with good reasons to stay. The rich vegetation and mud in the abandoned nests create new islands which support plant growth and eventually give roothold to trees, all of which provide attractive nesting places for a wide variety of creatures. Removing building material from the bottom of ponds makes the waterholes bigger and more attractive to those that prefer an aquatic environment. Birds and beasts and fish that come to the 'gator pool looking for a meal and are lulled into staying will probably become a meal themselves eventually, which is why alligators don't roam far. They don't need to. They have perfected a way to make their food come to them.

The alligator pools become even more important refuges in the dry season, when they often represent the only water for miles around. The 'gator's welcome mat is always out. After all, one never knows where the next meal is coming from.

Most of the alligator's victims never knows what hit them until they've been grabbed by the huge jaws and swallowed whole by their host, who knows very well how to bite, but has never learned to chew. The wily 'gator waits patiently submerged, except for its eyes, until the right victim comes along.

But not all the denizens of the Everglades try to make themselves unobtrusive. Some are downright showy. When the naturalist John James Audubon toured the Florida Bay area back in 1832 he couldn't contain his enthusiasm. "It was one of those sultry days which, in that portion of the country, exhibit towards evening the most glorious effulgence that can be conceived," he wrote. "The sun, now far advanced toward the horizon, still shone with full splendour, the ocean around glittered in its quiet beauty and the light fleecy clouds that here and there spotted the heavens seemed like flakes of snow margined with gold... Far away to seaward we spied a flock of flamingoes advancing in 'Indian line' with well-spread wings, outstretched necks and long legs directed backwards. Ah! reader, could you but know the emotions that then agitated my breast! I thought I had now reached the height of my expectations... I followed them with my eyes, watching as it were every beat of their wings." The only disappointment of the encounter was that the birds never got close enough for him to shoot any for his specimen collection. Later in his trip he was able to bag several, which he added to his collection of a thousand Florida birds. He even managed to capture some alive as gifts for his hosts in Charleston, the next stop on his journey back north.

Seeing wild flamingoes is much rarer today than it was in 1832, but since the first of them were bred in captivity in 1936, visitors have been guaranteed not to miss them. In spite of the exposure to the real thing, many insist on identifying an entirely different bird as a flamingo. The bird that causes the confusion is the one Floridians call the pink curlew, field guides call the roseate spoonbill and ornithologists call *ajaia ajaja*. By the end of the 1930s the world was ready to call these beautiful birds extinct. The North American version of the spoonbill is the only one of its species with bright colors. All their cousins, from Europe to Australia, are white. But for a while there, it seemed as though the color was more of a curse than a source of pride.

In the late years of the 19th century no woman who wanted to impress anyone would even think of not owning at least one plume of an American egret. When the National Audubon Society began a campaign to put the plume hunters out of business around the turn of the century, three of its wardens were killed in the attempt and the notoriety that resulted, finally, in a 1918 law that made it a crime even to own egret feathers, turned the attention of the profit-oriented hunters to other birds like the roseate spoonbill. Fortunately, feathered finery went out of fashion and the spoonbill, like the egret, was able to rise from the ashes to nearly the same levels that existed before all the silliness began. Man's encroachment on their territory has reduced them again, but they're in much less danger from the builders than they once were from the milliners.

The roseate spoonbills that winter in the Everglades fly in from Cuba in the early fall each year, and by November have finished building their nests in preparation for the hatching of the young. The blessed event always happens in mid-December, just in time for the surge of winter tourists.

But not many tourists see the babies, who stay safe and secure in their nests until about the end of January. Even if it isn't possible to see the little, white-headed fledglings, the spectacle the parents create in feeding them is a sight worth a trip into the swamp.

The great, rosy-pink birds swoop down on wings that extend as much as five feet, exposing patches of bright red, orange and yellow. Between visits by their parents, the more daring of the youngsters forage for themselves on the shore, often becoming food for hawks and falcons. But most are content to wait for the adults to arrive with their menu of predigested insects and larvae, which is literally spoon-fed to them. In the early weeks of life, adults feed any chicks who make a noise, regardless of parentage, but eventually, as if by a prearranged contract, the big birds stop feeding the young and they are forced to fend for themselves.

It doesn't take them long to figure out how it's done. They have developed a broad, spoon-shaped bill that makes it simple to gather the tiny, water-borne life they like to eat. They penetrate the bottom mud and swing their bill from side to side in an arc-like motion. When it feels like they have struck something good to eat, they pull the bill up sharply, trapping their prey and satisfying their appetitite. Because they are so big, and their prey so small, it's a full-time job.

But the activity adds to the joy of bird-watching in the Everglades, which is a never-ending job in itself. Up north, people who vaguely note that the birds that keep them company all summer and go "south" for the winter, are usually surprised to find their familiar friends in the Everglades when they themselves go south. Though not every migrating bird winds up in Southern Florida, the long stretch of water to the next landfall convinces many that it is just as well to stay in the Everglades, where the climate is great, the food plentiful and the company, admittedly not always friendly, is good.

Of course, people don't go to the Everglades to watch robins and woodpeckers, and once they've gotten over the surprise of finding them there, they don't even notice them. There are too many other more exotic species to catch their eye.

Among them is the wood ibis, the only stork native to the United States. It got its official designation as an ibis due to an 18th-century ornithologist, who studied it but couldn't make up his mind what sort of bird it really was. He first called it a wood pelican, but the more he looked at its non-expandable bill, the more he thought he must be wrong. He is to be forgiven, of course. He never expected to find a stork in North America. More unforgivable is the name given to it by native Floridians who insist on calling the bird a Spanish buzzard. Up in the Carolinas the confusion is worse. They call them gannets, a much different bird that looks more like a white cousin of the Canada goose than like the scaly-necked white wood ibises.

The huge spread of their black-tipped wings makes them a fascinating sight against the sky when they are in flight, but the real fun in watching these storks is at feeding time, which is almost all of the time. Most of the storks of the world spend a large part of their lives standing stiff-legged, watching for tasty morsels in shallow marshes. This branch of the family marches stiffly through the water in large groups, stirring up as much mud as they possibly can. Fish trying to escape the turmoil rise to near the surface, where they are stabbed by darting ibis beaks. In a short time, the surface of the water is littered with dead fish, snakes, frogs and baby alligators. It is only then that the feasting begins.

When the birds have gorged themselves they retreat to the shore where they rest in long rows with their breasts turned toward the sun. Soon, as if by signal, they all take flight at once, spiraling upward as high as 2500 feet and then they glide on the warm air currents for an hour or more until their meal is completely digested. In the process they have put on a show almost unequalled in nature.

Because they are such good gliders, they are able to range as far as 20 miles to find likely feeding ponds and marshes. But, like so many other Everglades natives, their range isn't enough to keep up with the changes the hand of man has wrought. In the late 1950s flocks of them abandoned Florida completely and were reported as far north as Connecticut and as far west as Wyoming, looking for marshland that might have enough fish to keep their huge appetites satisfied.

But since then they've moved back to the warmer Gulf Coast and the Carolinas. Some winter in California and Arizona, but their favorite nesting grounds are still in the Southern Florida marshes, where the battle continues against man's appetitie for warm sun and blue water. Man will probably win in the end, of course. But in the process, we are in danger of losing one of South Florida's most beautiful natural sights.

A member of the local bird population that sometimes surprises Everglades visitors is the bald eagle. Though the common perception is that most of them live in high, rocky crags along the Continental Divide, the fact is that, except for Alaska, Florida is home to more specimens of America's national bird than any other state.

Even though some of their western relatives do live in high mountain aeries, eagles are quite at home in the Everglades region, where the highest point of land is less than 20 feet above sea level. What they like better than height is water or, more accurately, they like the fish that live in the water. They build their huge nests in the highest trees they can find, to be sure, but in the Florida Keys they compromise with black mangroves that rarely reach higher than 30 feet. Their nests are hard to miss. Made of sticks and bark, they are rectangular structures as high as nine feet and as long as five feet. This huge apartment is the cozy first home of the baby eagles that are the product of just two eggs usually laid each year during the winter.

The nesting pair will stay together all their lives, mating year after year until one of them no longer returns to the nest. A mature bird's wingspread can be as wide as seven feet and its body four feet long. Seeing one in flight is awe-inspiring. Apparently it's a frightening experience to some other birds, though. The bald eagle is one of nature's great fish-catchers, but it saves effort frequently by forcing smaller osprey to drop their catches, which it then snatches in midair.

The eagle's legendary eyesight is partly responsible for such feats. But if they see well, they don't always seem to know what they are seeing. All sorts of junk has been found in their nests, from tennis balls to light bulbs to soft drink cans. It may be an attempt to adapt to the new Florida lifestyle, of course, but more likely it is an indication that they will eat just about anything. They regularly dine on small mammals and turtles, too, seem worth the challenge. But except for fish, their preference seems to be for other birds. They'll even eat seagulls, who themselves will eat anything the tide washes up and probably aren't very tasty.

For all their great size and menacing appearance, bald eagles are usually docile when their nests are disturbed. Because of that the representation of the bird on the Great Seal of the United States is probably more accurately reflected in the talon that holds an olive branch than the one with the bundle of arrows. They protest intrusions by circling high overhead, making an odd yapping sound. It's almost embarrassing considering the wide mythology about screaming eagles. The scream is actually more like a whimper. Our national bird is like a beautiful sportscar with a squeaky horn.

As the symbol of a mighty nation, though, the Founding Fathers probably couldn't have found a creature more beautiful. It wasn't a capricious decision, but rather the result of long, careful debate. The grand old man among them, Benjamin Franklin, held out for a much different bird, the turkey, which roamed wild in every one of the original states. Their range extended all the way to the Dakotas, in fact, but Franklin had no way of knowing that.

The small species of wild turkey that nests in the Everglades hammocks is known to ornithologists as "Osceola" for the Seminole chief. It has nothing to do with the current fashion of using the word "turkey" to describe a dullard. On the contrary, the name was given to this great game bird as a tribute. During the three-month mating season, beginning around the end of January, they show a fierce nature that is sometimes surprising. The rest of the year they have a talent for hiding in thickets or at the tops of high trees.

Another bird that isn't related to the wild turkey, but shares its name is the water turkey, often known as the snakebird. In the air, their long necks and bills and their fan-shaped tail make them incredibly beautiful. But a perching snakebird is probably the most ungraceful of all the creatures that live in the marshes. When they're frightened they drop like a falling branch and sink like lead into the water. A little bit later they poke their head out to see if the danger is past. When they're looking for food, though, they don't plunge into the water from the air but dive from the surface and swim underwater spearing fish. Once they've had enough of that they retire to the shore where they spread their wings to dry.

Every one of the hundreds of different kinds of birds that live or spend time in the River of Grass has figured out its own way to stay alive and well-fed. Pelicans, for instance, dive from 30 feet in the air with their wings spread, emerging upwind with a fish in their pouch. Their constant companions, laughing gulls often go along for the ride and land on the emerging pelican's head to rob it of its catch.

Herons, ibises, egrets and other long legged birds stand patiently at the edge of ponds and marshes hoping a frog or a snake will come along before dinner time. One rare member of the family, an import from Africa by way of British Guiana, is known as the cattle egret because of its odd habit of following herds of grazing cattle. Unlike most of the birds of southern Florida, they have been attracted there by the presence of man.

The winter population of ducks and geese from the frozen north is incredible, but at least one close relative of the mallard stays in the Florida marshes all year 'round. And not all come from the north; dozens of species fly in from places like Bermuda and Central America to add their voices to the din around the fresh water ponds, not to mention providing great sport for people who get a kick out of shooting them.

Sightseers in the Everglades region who take to the roads early in the morning are often appalled by the huge number of dead animals killed the night before by speeding cars. Later in the day they have usually disappeared thanks to nature's own clean-up crew, the huge vultures who are no doubt grateful for man's carelessness. The locals call these huge, ugly birds "buzzards," a name that fits a quite different member of the hawk family. But, as the saying goes, you can call them anything but late for dinner. They spend much of their time making great, lazy circles in the air looking for food below. When one spots something and lands to claim it, it is certain that a whole flock of them will soon be sharing the feast.

Though their favorite food is decomposing animal matter, vultures also like heron eggs, and have been known to capture live farm animals.

Other kites, falcons and hawks are more likely to be shooed away by nervous farmers, but none of them considers a chicken as much a delicacy as a frog or small snake. They like some of the other local birds, too, and even without farms to raid, the choice is almost too wide to be believed.

Every inch of the Everglades teems with life, and for many birds the teardrop-shaped hammocks provide the right shelter and the right hunting ground to sustain their own life. The hammocks are covered with hardwood trees like mahogany, live oak and gumbo limbo. The leaves they drop are washed away in heavy rains and their chemical effect on the nearby limestone creates deep freshwater channels around them. The channels not only help support life, but usually keep the hammock secure from all but the wildest of fires.

The environment inside the hammock is as

different from the outside sawgrass prairie as it is from downtown Miami. The thick canopy of trees shuts out the bright sun; the soft bed of leaves underfoot makes walking a sensual pleasure. Most hammocks provide shelter for deer and raccoons, for otters and other small creatures. It is where you'd be most likely to meet one of the very few remaining cougars or at least a bobcat. But the animal life is far less exciting than the trees, plants and flowers that make the average Everglades hammock often seem like the Garden of Eden.

Of all the exotic growth, the most unusual is probably the air plant known as the strangler fig. It is planted by passing birds in the tops of trees, but it's obvious that it prefers to put its roots into the ground. As it grows, the roots dangle downward, eventually clinging to the tree's trunk for support. But in return for the support, the growing roots stangle the tree in great coils until it eventually dies, making space for the fig itself to grow. Since it starts out as an air plant, any damage from a storm or a passing animal does nothing more than start a new plant which continues the deadly process.

Not every hammock is the same, of course. In fact, no two are exactly alike. Many contain old live oak trees festooned with Spanish moss, others are covered with mahogany forests. Some have open clearings in the center, complete with open fresh water ponds that are playgrounds for otters and hunting grounds for long-legged birds. Most have dense covers of ferns and orchids and the trees are decorated with beautiful bromeliads, air plants which, unlike the strangler fig, seem to have no other purpose in life than to add a touch of beauty to their host.

But none of them has quite the same beauty as the liguus tree snail, a creature who wouldn't live anywhere but on an Everglades hammock. There are many different varieties, each with its own distinct shell markings. As is the case with just about everything else in the Everglades, some of the varieties have become extinct and the rest endangered because people like to take the colorful shells home with them.

Whatever they do with them when they get them there, the setting can't be as beautiful as the tree snail's own home. They cling to the bark of trees which is already covered with colorful lichens, the snail's favorite food. Tree snails are only active in the wet season, during which time they lay their eggs in the ground near the base of their host trees. During dry times they build a transparent cover over themselves and go dormant until the rain comes again.

At almost any season, snakes are a part of the variety of life on the hammocks as well as everywhere else in the Glades. There are, in fact, 26 different kinds of snakes in the Everglades, only four of which are poisonous. You can tell which is which by looking them in the eye. Non-poisonous snakes have round pupils. But if you'd rather not, rest assured that the odds are that the snake you're looking at probably won't hurt you. Even rattlesnakes and water moccasins would rather not waste their venom on anything as large as a human which, after all, is quite inedible. On the other hand, the best policy is to avoid them.

Snakes, like many other inhabitants of the Everglades, have long since learned to avoid man even if they can't avoid the effects of what man has done to their environment.

But if man has been busy destroying the northern part of their domain, nature has been busy, too, building up the southern end. The difference is that nature isn't driven by such a tight time schedule.

Much of the natural reclamation is being done by groves of mangrove trees which anchor themselves in mud washed ashore in storms. The red mangrove rises up on an exposed network of long, curving roots which extend out from the bottom almost as far as the branches above. As new roots are sent out, the tree gets a kind of mobility that allows it to move further out into the water. Meanwhile, mud and debris collect around the roots creating new land. The process is enhanced by the fruit of the tree, which doesn't fall off until is has grown an eight-inch seedling. The fruit itself acts as a tiny boat that carries the seedling to another mudbank, where its destiny will be to help create another spongy island.

The work has been going on for thousands of years, and some scientists say that more than two-thirds of the land area in Everglades National Park was at the bottom of the sea when the Egyptians were building their pyramids. But even at that rate, it will be a long, long time before the southern tip of Florida bumps into Cuba.

Mangroves are able to tolerate salt water and their roots can stay submerged for months at a time. Though they are usually the only form of plant life in their territory, their falling leaves add nutrients to the water that support all sorts of life, from shrimps and oysters to the birds that eat them. The sandy islands they create provide nesting grounds for salt water amphibians and for the mammals that thrive on their eggs. The small fish that breed among the mangrove roots feed the big fish that make sport fishing such a great attraction on the Southern coast of Florida.

Further inland, the work of the red mangrove is taken over by its near relative, the black mangrove. Even deeper in the interior, white mangroves take over, and their job of anchoring the soil is aided by other plants and trees that can tolerate a salty environment. Eventually, of course, the salt will leach away and the land will be truly reclaimed.

All of these plants and trees get rid of salt through their leaves. The ones that haven't mastered the trick need to be able to get along with little or no water, which is why cactus and prickly pear add to the wide variety of life in parts of the Everglades.

Much of the water and natural debris that passes from the Everglades into the mangrove forests passes first through the Big Cypress Swamp, a 2,400-square-mile area of deep ponds and long sloughs filled with cypress trees that give it an air of brooding mystery.

The cypress is a close relative of the California redwood that has adapted itself to the acid soils and vast water of the swamps of Southeastern United States. Its tall trunks and branches festooned with Spanish moss ideally fit the popular image of a swamp, which is why so many people are reassured to find the Big Cypress Swamp when they visit the Everglades.

The big trees are able to put their roots down under water because they send out stump-like growths, called "knees," which rise above the surface to help the tree breathe. Other plants, like water hyacinths, take advantage of the shelter of the tall trees to thrive in the deep, dark pools, adding to the classic, mysteriously beautiful image.

It provides a perfect breeding ground for deer and Florida panthers, and the only black bears left in the wild in Florida find refuge in the swamp. The trees also provide perches for all sorts of bird life. If the natural environment isn't protective enough, about a third of the swamp is under the control of the National Park Service, which restrains over-eager hunters, developers and their kind.

The eastern side of the Everglades was once separated from the coast by a forest of pine trees about five miles wide. Most of the forest has been replaced by housing as Greater Miami has become greater still, but fortunately some of it has been left and protected within the National Park.

In most parts of the world, pine forests are gradually replaced by hardwoods largely by the action of natural fires. The Everglades pinelands have had more than their share of fires over the centuries, but the slash pine that grows there has figured out a way to beat the system. Its bark is arranged in tightly rolled layers which allow the tree to continue sending food from leaves to roots even when one or more of them are burned away. Bushier plants like the palmetto survive fires by sending out new growth from unburned roots. Only hardwoods are destroyed and so the slash pine forest never changes. Except when they bring in the bulldozers.

But in spite of bulldozers and dredges and a lack of respect for the laws of nature almost unequalled in the history of mankind, the Everglades flows on. It will never be the same as it was when Spanish explorers began dodging alligators, or when the Seminole retreated to the protective cover of its hammocks. But the time when nobody seemed to care is behind us now and it is likely that our grandchildren may have a chance to see and marvel at wonders that exist nowhere else on earth but in the Everglades. On the other hand, there is no guarantee. Life in the Glades is fragile and the lust to build is still flourishing in Southern Florida.

What happens next is up to us. Deep in the Everglades you get the impression of a place where time is standing still. But the reality is apparent at night, when the lights of nearby cities can be seen through the inky darkness. We can only hope that enough people have seen the light and are willing to fight back to keep them from getting any closer.

Right: an anhinga spreads its wings to dry.

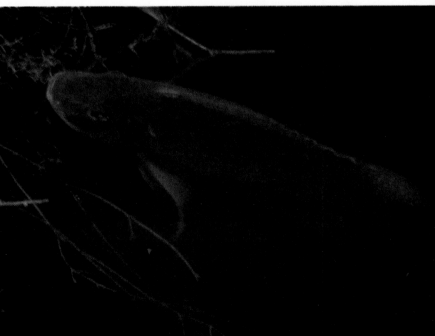

Top: the broad, blunt snout of an alligator, one of the many which inhabit the Everglades' complex system of lakes, sloughs and swamps. The common moorhen (left and facing page) is found in freshwater ponds and marshes and feeds at the edge of open water, ready to seek shelter in bordering vegetation if disturbed.

Facing page: boardwalks, such as that on the Anhinga Trail (top), allow visitors to explore Everglades National Park close at hand, but safely and with the least disturbance to wildlife. (Bottom) the Royal Palm Visitors' Center helps provide the park's thousands of visitors with information and services. Top left: an alligator uses the sun's heat to raise its body temperature, and (top right) a great blue heron watches for fish in the shallows. The anhinga (above) swims completely submerged in pursuit of its prey, using its sharp bill to spear fish, snakes, frogs and crustaceans. Inadequate oil glands fail to protect the anhinga's feathers from becoming waterlogged, and it must spread its sodden wings to dry in the sun. Overleaf: sunrise beyond a stand of slash pines.

Facing page: (top) a great blue heron stands motionless and ready to strike (bottom). Left: red and green bracts on the flower stalk of the wild-pine, a bromeliad which usually grows in the bark of the cypress. The Anhinga Trail (top) passes over the Taylor Slough (above), a slow-moving, freshwater, marshy river. On a smaller scale, sloughs form where water gathers in shallow troughs in the limestone bedrock, and may retain much-needed water even into the winter dry season.

Below: anhingas among the twisted branches of a pond apple tree, and (overleaf and bottom left) alligators seen from the Anhinga Trail (bottom right). Bottom center: a great blue heron watches for fish beside the broad, lance-shaped leaves and violet flower-spikes of pickerelweed. Right: alligator and pond lily.

This page: roseate spoonbills feeding in the saltwater shallows of the coastal Everglades. The spoonbill's distinctive, flattened bill provides it with a broad area through which to sift mud and water for the small marine life on which it feeds. Facing page: (top) a freshwater pond in Taylor Slough, on the Anhinga Trail, where (bottom) a common moorhen feeds on aquatic vegetation and pondlife.

Left: young anhingas on a characteristically untidy nest, shielded by dense stands of bamboo. Below: visitors at the Royal Palm Center, and (bottom) a male anhinga, nearly three feet long from bill tip to tail tip.

The anhinga's distinctive plumage (right) can become so sodden and bedraggled during the underwater stalking of its food that it cannot fly, and has to clamber and claw its way to a safe perch. Facing page: anhinga preening, and (bottom) with back-feathers fluffed, wings outstretched and tail fanned to dry. Below: immature great blue heron.

Left: sunrise beyond a tall slash pine, and (bottom) dwarf cypresses silhouetted. Below: Snake Bight mudflats, on the north shore of Florida Bay. The dry, cracked surface layer is easily broken to reveal a foot or two of mud. Overleaf: devastation following a forest fire. Everglades' pinelands owe their existence to the periodic invasions of fire, which regulate the numbers of broad-leaved hardwoods growing beneath the pines. Unchecked, hardwoods would eventually shade out the pine seedlings and become established in their stead.

Both wild and manmade fires (facing page and below) played a major role in shaping the Everglades. The Seminole Indians burned the prairies to flush out game, to kill ticks and rattlesnakes, or to make new grazing for their cattle and ponies. The white ranchers who displaced them continued and increased the practice. Fire is now employed to conserve the landscape rather than change it; for example, at Corkscrew Swamp controlled burning is used to stop the encroachment of the coastal willow onto the central marsh. Right: ragwort flourishes on land cleared by a burn, Corkscrew Swamp. Bottom: dwarf cypress and sawgrass.

Big Cypress Swamp (these pages) in the northwest of the Everglades is not, strictly speaking, a swamp, but a closely interrelated complex of sandy islands supporting slash pines, mixed hardwood hammocks, wet prairies, dry prairies, marshes, and estuarine mangrove forests. Left: an airboat tour of Big Cypress Swamp National Preserve. Below: royal palms at Ochobee, and (bottom left) wet prairie. Bottom right: islands of cabbage palm and saw palmettos dot dry prairieland in Big Cypress Swamp.

Top: a strand of slash pines lining open water, Big Cypress Swamp. Left: new vegetation quickly reclaims ground cleared by a burn. Above: floating waterweeds on the surface of a freshwater pond. Among the species that flourish in such environments are the tiny-leaved duckweed, watermeal or wolffia, and the floating fern or azolla. Facing page: (top) cabbage palms, and (bottom) mangrove forest along the saltwater, coastal fringe of Big Cypress Swamp.

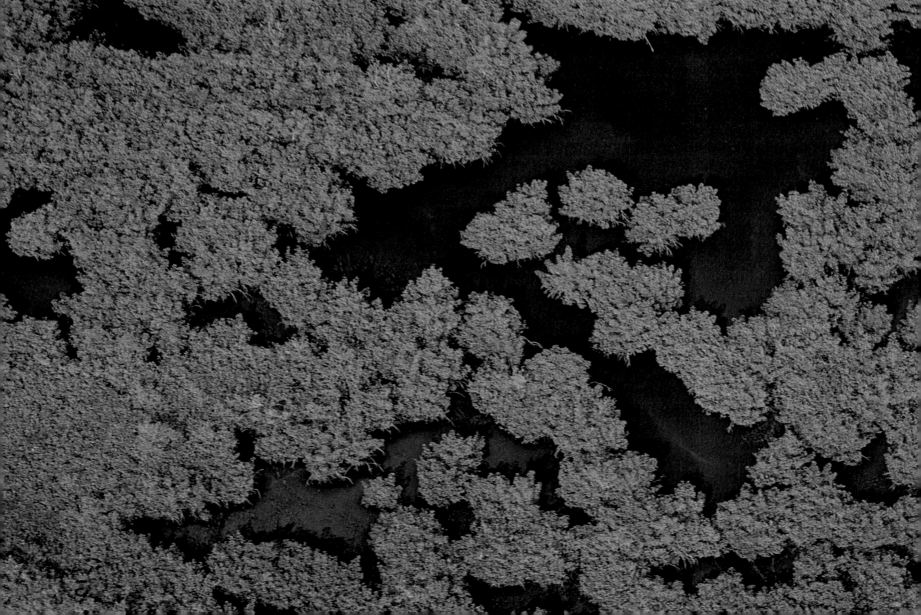

Alligators (these pages) mate in April and May, during which time the bulls will fight (facing page, bottom). The female builds a nest of weeds and rotting leaves, raised into a mound above the water, where she lays up to 60 eggs in late May or early June. Incubated by the heat of the sun and the decomposing vegetation, the eggs hatch after about 65 days to release miniature alligators about nine inches long. Below: young alligator. Overleaf: Trafford Lake, near Immokalee.

Left: a great egret, and (bottom) a river otter emerging from the weeds. Below: a slough and heads of palms and other trees above the sawgrass prairie. Facing page: (top) salt-resistant grasses in the winter dry season, and (bottom) an island of cabbage palms and saw palmetto. Overleaf: freshwater channels dissect Big Cypress Swamp.

Facing page: (bottom) evening on Lake Trafford, near Immokalee in Big Cypress Swamp (top). Top: a stand of slash pines and the blue spikes of pickerelweed lining slow-moving freshwater near Immokalee. Left: a great blue heron amongst overhanging willow, and (above) an alligator.

Facing page: (top) mangroves on Rabbit Key, in Ten Thousand Islands, and (bottom) Louisiana heron, snowy egret, and immature roseate spoonbills feeding in Big Cypress Swamp. Left: a brown pelican, and (bottom) a great egret. Below: seedling red mangrove, oyster bar and groves of red mangrove trees, their long, exposed roots harboring mud, sand and debris to form growing islands, Ten Thousand Islands.

Facing page: (top) red mangroves grow in shallow salt water at Ten Thousand Islands, supported on curved prop roots. The stems of the saw palmetto (bottom), usually below ground, may emerge as short, reclining trunks supporting many leaf bases, from which grow stiff, deeply-divided leaves. Right: charred saw palmettos, and (bottom) burnt woodland of saw palmettos and slash pines. The moist bark of pines and palmettos gives them a degree of resistance to fire, and they can recover and flourish quickly following occasional, limited burns. Below: shoveler ducks and double-crested cormorants.

Below: Chokoloskee Bay. Left: double-crested cormorants, and (below center) an adult and an immature brown pelican. Bottom: the beginnings of a small mangrove island at Ten Thousand Islands, where (overleaf) roseate spoonbills feed in the shallows among sapling red and black mangroves.

Previous pages: Ten Thousand Islands, off Florida's west coast. (Left) sunset, (right, top) the spreading maze of mangrove forests, and (right, bottom) a young red mangrove tree, rooted in the raised bed offered by an oyster bar.

Above: a little blue heron watching the weed-covered surface, and (facing page) a yellow-crowned night-heron. Left: the Turner River. Overleaf: (left, top) the Rod and Gun Club, (left, bottom) a church, and (right) boat moored beside a pink poui tree, all in Everglades City.

Chokoloskee Island (left) was formed by the accumulation of a great shell mound, and once supported a community of the Calusa Indians, predecessors of the Seminole. Below: Everglades City Hall and the old Everglades Bank, and (bottom center) Ochopee Post Office, the smallest post office in America. Bottom left: fishing, and (bottom right) feeding the pelicans. Overleaf: coconut palms in Everglades City.

Above: a Louisiana heron, generally found on saltwater shores, and (far right, center) a green heron, shorter necked than most types of heron. Top right: an alligator waits, almost entirely submerged, for unwary prey. Top: canoeing, and (right) a tangle of red mangrove roots on the upper Turner River, near Chokoloskee.

Below: red mangroves near Everglades City, and (bottom) alligators in Everglades Wonder Garden. Right: serrated fronds of wild Boston fern and the long, sword-like leaves of strap fern growing on fallen logs and at the base of bald cypress trees. The conical, bark-covered cypress knees, offshoots from the roots of the cypresses, may help the trees to "breathe", or provide them with structural support where they grow in unstable ground.

Previous pages: the Turner River, overhung by red mangroves. Left and below: a wary river otter. Otters feed on a variety of small aquatic animals, including fish, which they may catch through working together as a team. Facing page: (top) the green heron is common by both salt and freshwater, and is found more frequently than other herons in small ponds and along wooded streams. Bottom: red mangrove roots.

The tribal culture of the Miccosukee, a branch of the Seminole, is preserved in static, commercialized form in the Miccosukee Indian Village (bottom) and Culture Center on the Tamiami Trail. Below: head of a totem pole, and (left and bottom) Seminole *chickees*, huts of cypress poles roofed with palmetto and thatch. Facing page: a Miccosukee woman produces traditional goods for sale. Overleaf: airboat expedition from the Miccosukee Village.

Traditional alligator wrestling, (top left and left) in the Miccosukee Village, and (top and above) on the Alligator Alley reservation, is a favorite tourist attraction. Facing page: traditional goods, some produced with the aid of modern methods. Overleaf: an airboat skims across water lettuce, piloted by a Miccosukee Indian guide.

Corkscrew Swamp Sanctuary (these pages) is a remnant wilderness area of 11,000 acres, and includes America's largest remaining strand of virgin bald cypresses. Facing page: (top) the broad leaves of fire flags, and tiny-leaved, floating water-fern. (Bottom) bromeliads growing low on the trunks of pond cypresses, and (above) a strand of bald cypresses, supported on broad buttresses. Pond and bald cypresses were thought to be distinct varieties, but are now widely considered as site adaptations of the same tree. Left: a white-tailed deer. Overleaf: (left, top) monarch butterfly and (left, bottom) boardwalk in Corkscrew Swamp Sanctuary. (Right) a pond-slider turtle.

Previous pages: Spanish moss, a hanging epiphyte, Corkscrew Swamp. Left: nesting wood storks, the adults with dark, unfeathered heads, and (below) a great egret. Bottom: a dense stand of bald cypresses, and (facing page) the boardwalk, in Corkscrew Swamp Sanctuary.

Previous pages: the feathery leaves of the cypress (left) are shed in winter. (Right) wet prairie. Below: a hungry raccoon, (right) an alligator, and (bottom) bald cypress trees, in Corkscrew Swamp Sanctuary. Overleaf: great egrets and a wood stork feed among water lettuce, a free-floating plant which virtually covers many of the deeper lakes of Corkscrew Swamp.

Corkscrew Swamp Sanctuary (these pages) was established with the aid of the National Audubon Society, which is now responsible for the conservation and management of the area. To protect both swamp and visitors the Society constructed a boardwalk extending for more than a mile – over ponds covered with water lettuce (facing page and above), wet prairie (top), and past air plants growing thickly on the trunks of bald cypresses (right). Broad buttresses, which can grow to be eight to ten feet across, help the cypress trees' shallow root system to support their height in unstable ground.

The raccoon (bottom right), seen here hunting warily in Corkscrew Swamp Sanctuary, flourishes in almost every habitat to be found in the Everglades. Right and bottom: alligators emerge from the water to sun themselves, thus raising their externally-controlled body temperature. Below and bottom: dense surface-coverings of water lettuce, a major source of the dead vegetation continually being laid down as a rich, organic peat.

Previous pages: sunset over the Gulf of Mexico. Far left, bottom left and bottom right: Italian-style houses surround a marina in Naples. Further south, Marco Island, the largest of the Ten Thousand Islands, has been transformed from wilderness into a complex of orderly streets, canals and luxury accommodation (left and below). Overleaf: Vanderbilt Beach, north of Naples.

Seven miles of wide, palm-lined beach (left and above) and good fishing (facing page, bottom) make Naples, at the far northwestern edge of the Everglades, an attractive vacation resort. Facing page: (top) the order wreaked by a multi-million-dollar development project on Marco Island. Overleaf: Naples' architecture lives up to its less pristine Italian namesake.

Left: a forest of air-absorbing black mangrove roots, or pneumatophores, which grow vertically from the trees' submerged lateral roots. Bottom: grove of cypress, palm and saw palmetto, and (bottom right) a pond slider turtle basking, both to warm itself and to dry and kill back algae and leeches which may be living on its skin and shell. Below: a strangler fig, which has grown around, smothered and now replaced the host oak tree.

The plain of saw grass and spike rush that constitutes Shark River Slough is set with dense hammocks of tropical hardwood trees (above and overleaf). These occur where the waterflow slows almost to a standstill and seedlings are able to gain footholds on raised areas of limestone. These develop into roughly circular islands, consisting of combinations of live oak, mahogany, cocoplum and gumbo limbo, and may enclose solution holes (above), where the limestone has been dissolved down below the water table. Left: saw palmetto on a trail in Shark Valley. Facing page: double-crested cormorants in a slash pine.

Right: Shark River Slough, a slow-moving sheet of water which flows over the almost imperceptible gradient of the low, limestone plain. Sawgrass, a sedge, grows from a layer of peat resting on the limestone, and owes its name to the fine, sharp teeth along the midrib and edges of the leaves. Below and bottom left: alligators, and (bottom right) white ibis feeding in Shark River Slough.

Near the coast the freshwater cypress, pine and saw-grass landscapes give way to dense, saltwater mangrove forest (facing page, top). Three varieties of mangrove generally appear in a well-established pattern, white mangroves growing furthest inland and having few breathing roots; black mangroves, with their forests of pneumatophores, occupying the Everglades' tidal zones; and red mangroves, (facing page, bottom) supported on labyrinthine prop roots, continually colonizing the fringes of the ocean. Top: a water moccasin, and (left and above) a demonstration of how to handle a snake without danger to either party.

G ator holes, such as that (below) at Big Cypress Swamp, provide vital catchments for the fast-disappearing water during the winter dry season, and sustain a wide variety of wildlife until the spring rains. Left: pond apple trees, and (bottom pictures) a water moccasin. Overleaf: (left, and right, top) mangroves. The anhinga, (right, bottom) is known also as the snakebird by virtue of its long, sleek head and neck, which occasionally protrude above water level as it swims in pursuit of fish.

Top left: expanses of low-growing saltwort on the coastal prairie, and (top right) a narrow waterway smothered with water lettuce. Above: an immature white ibis. Left and right: white mangroves, with pale bark, no prop roots and few breathing roots, grow to the landward of other mangroves and mark the gradual change from the freshwater Everglades to the saltwater tidal areas.

Raccoons (previous pages and these pages) hunt, forage and scavenge for a wide variety of foods, including fish, oysters, insects, small mammals, birds and their eggs, and many fruits and plants. With the onset of the dry season in November, their abundant food supplies are drastically reduced, and, together with their prey and predators, they search the dried-up prairies even for water. By the time the first spring rains come, in about May, many have died of thirst and starvation.

In order to reclaim Everglades land and render it fit for agriculture the annual extremes of flood and drought, which create the unique balance and character of Everglades life, are cancelled out in comprehensive programs of drainage and irrigation (top and facing page, top). Thus regulated, land just outside Everglades National Park produces squashes (right) and tomatoes (above). Facing page: (bottom) cracked earth of a dry prairie.

Facing page: an extensive strand of slash pines. Pinewoods flourish only in elevated, and therefore comparatively dry, areas containing bare limestone outcrops, and may root in soil-containing solution holes in the limestone. Above: a bromeliad, a type of epiphyte or air plant. Non-parasitic, epiphytes use trees purely for support, in order to avoid the inhospitable extremes of wet and dry that exist at ground level. Top: a natural tunnel enclosing the road to Flamingo, and (right) anhinga in the branches of a southern willow. Overleaf: mature red mangrove forest near Everglades City.

The old road to Flamingo (left), now traveled only on foot, is being fast encroached upon by the surrounding forest. Below: sunset over prairieland of sawgrass and dwarf cypresses. A site adaptation of the variant known as pond cypress, these low trees are stunted by poor, thin soil and fluctuating water levels. Bottom: wild pine, an epiphyte member of the pineapple family. Overleaf: moonrise over sawgrass and dwarf cypress prairie.

Flamingo, originally a small fishing settlement, now provides tourist facilities for visitors to Everglades National Park. Below: canoeing out of Flamingo marina (facing page, top), where a brown pelican stands sentinel (left). Bottom and facing page, bottom: Madeira Bay. Overleaf: (left and right, top) flamingoes, and (right, bottom) a white peacock, in Parrot Jungle, Miami.

Madeira Bay (facing page) lies east of Flamingo on the north shore of Florida Bay. Right: a brown pelican in summer plumage, and (below) the white variant of the great blue heron, found only in salt water from southern Biscayne Bay around the coast to Everglades City. Discovered by John James Audubon, the great white heron will breed with the great blue, and now both birds are considered to be the same species. Overleaf: sunset over Key Largo.

Top: the white variant of the great blue heron at Eco pond (above), and (right) a cattle egret. Facing page: (top) drought-stricken marshland, and (bottom) glasswort, a succulent which flourishes in the saltwater soil of the coastal prairie.

Offspring of the largest of North American herons, an immature great blue heron (bottom) may grow to an adult height of four feet. The Louisiana heron (left) feeds along saltwater shores, in company with the white ibis (below). White ibis often congregate in large flocks, flying in long lines or in V-formation. Different types of heron and other water birds will readily share both feeding and nesting grounds, and noisy, untidy mixed rookeries are a distinctive feature of cypress and mangrove forests.

Slider turtles (bottom right) dig themselves into the moist undersoil at the onset of the dry season, and there survive the drought in a state of aestivation – a condition akin to hibernation, but not as deep or sustained. During particularly severe drought even the reservoir-like 'gator holes may prove insufficient, and alligators (remaining pictures) will aestivate in damp dens adjoining their dried-up waterholes.

Facing page: (top) a common moorhen, which feeds along the edges of freshwater marshes and lakes. The lingering of saltwater in the soil of the coastal prairies makes them hospitable only to salt-tolerant plants, including water-retaining succulents such as saltwort (facing page, bottom and below). Right: primrose willow, and (bottom) roseate spoonbills roosting at Eco Pond.

Left: the white variant of the great blue heron, (bottom) a great egret, and (below) reflections in Eco Pond. Overleaf: US Highway 41, known as the Tamiami Trail, runs from east to west across the top of Everglades National Park.

Left: water lettuce spreading over a pond in Loxahatchee National Wildlife Reserve, and (bottom center) cypress knees. Bottom left: cattle on land lost to pasture in the Devil's Garden. Below: an immature little blue heron, and (bottom right) an anhinga producing its harsh alarm cry.

Facing page: fans of saw palmetto in dense woodland at Fahkahatchee, and (top) dwarf cypresses beside the Ingraham Trail. Right: duckweed covers the mud of a fast-drying pond. The purple gallinule (above), though more colorful, is very similar to the common moorhen in its habits and hen-like call. Overleaf: sunrise above a stand of slash pines.